intentionally blank

intentionally blank

Defeating Your Giants

Rev Albert O Olorunleye

Jesus Joy Publishing

Published and printed in Great Britain in 2015 by
Jesus Joy Publishing.

ISBN 978-1-90797-144-0

Jesus Joy Publishing
is a division of Eklegein Ltd
www.jesusjoypublishing.co.uk
20150929

Dedication

I would like to dedicate this book to my role model - Jesus Christ of Nazareth.

Also to my dear and lovely wife, Victoria Olorunleye, and my children - for their support and dedication to the work of the ministry at large.

Finally, to all the members of CAC Kings Tabernacle International.

Preface

This book contains some of my years of Christian life and ministry experiences, as well as those challenges that must be faced to be a successful Christian and a leader. These experiences may not be considered as an ideal standard for all Christians and leaders to be successful as Christians but it can equip Christians and leaders with necessary knowledge and tools to help develop themselves and other Christians.

Giants in this book are the types of problems, challenges, troubles or hindrances that you can face as faithful Christians, leaders, and workers in the church or in your career ladder to success. It may be forces of evil that wage war against your soul or people in your life that have betrayed you, disappointed you or even wrecked your life in some way. These giants could be your ignorance, wrong relationships and associations, unbelief, and disappointment from people you trust and love. It is normal to face these giants in life but dangerous to ignore them as they pose risks to your success and breakthrough.

No Christian can come to the point of claiming success and spiritual achievement without passing through those things that we perceive on our journeys as mountains or hindrances which were not actually mountains, but an open door to success.

Whosoever is looking for success in life must be ready to face and surmount giants. Jesus came across his own giants but those giants were crushed and victory was achieved for all humanity.

The Bible is an inexhaustible book of wisdom and it paves the way without bias, stating nothing less than the truth to give light to your life. Therefore, all Scriptures become inductive, instructive and corrective to equip you for all good works and to take steps to demolish all attacks of giants that come your way. Hence you will achieve the destiny which God has embedded in you to achieve at creation.

God is a God of purpose and He has created you for a particular purpose with specific reasons in mind before creating you. You must realise that you are not a purposeless being but a rational being who can bring forth the marvellous glory of God. This is the reason why God the Creator is the only God that you must worship at all times. It is sinful for anyone to worship other creatures created by Jehovah God. I hope you will ponder carefully on the Scriptures given in this book and some illustrations that follow them for your edification.

The purpose of your existence on earth is to represent God as His image, and to live a life full of the power of the Holy Spirit. Through obedience to the commandments of God, you can achieve His purpose and live out your true identity as a child of God. You must totally rely on the power of the Holy Spirit in your life to do great exploits for God as His servant and as a child of God.

The purpose of God in creating you in His image is for you to represent His true identity on earth. God is a God of love, integrity, endurance and peace, and above all, He hears and listens. He listens to His children and wants them to enjoy His good provisions to the fullest. He is a God of abundance and the life He has given you was given in abundance.

Acknowledgements

I thank Almighty Jehovah, the Father of all creation, who has endowed me with knowledge and wisdom to write this book and for the inspiration and understanding received from Him to accomplished the task. I thank my Jehovah God who sees me through all the challenges in my difficult and dark hours and for illuminating my journey through the dark side of life and enabling me to experience victory over all my obstacles; to Him be the glory forever.

Amen.

It would be an incomplete record if I failed to mention the assistance received from men and woman of probity in the persons of Pius A. Omonijo, Victor Mijebi Sulaiman, Victor A. Olorunleye, Dr. Kent and Victoria Olorunleye who have contributed greatly from start to finish in the compilation of this book. A million thanks to them for what they have done.

Contents

Chapter 1

The Origin of Giants

The First Created Man

God made you in His image as a tripartite creature. That means that you are a spirit being with soul and flesh. Adam, the first man God created was not without a giant and that giant was the devil. Giants are common to human beings and overcoming them form very important milestones to gaining our freedom and achieving greatness. You can never be great without giants coming on your way. As the adage says, *'no crown without conflict and no medal without a race to run.'*

The first human being was purposefully created to represent God and rule over all other things that God created. To be created in the image of God implies that you are representing the active intention of God in tangible ways. No one has seen God at any time because He is an invisible God who needed the visible man to manage the affairs of His entire creation.

God allowed Adam to give names to all that He created in the Garden of Eden. God's power of attorney that was given to Adam was so great that whatever names he gave to the creatures, were their names forever. [Genesis 2:9]

God created man in His image. Therefore there is no need for any other image to be created by man. Whosoever creates any image and worships it, contravenes the command of God and His wrath is kindled towards that person. [Exodus 20:4-6]

What then is the image of God? We should always seek to make the right interpretation of what God means when He made the statement. It is a statement of intent that God made in order to carry out His creative works.

The word 'Image of God' simply embodies the moral, ethical, and intellectual abilities of God in the human being He first created. The attributes of the man created was based on these abilities and they were greatly valued by God. Human beings were created to have dominion and authority to rule over all other creatures in a way that would bring to light, God's plan and purpose. [Genesis 1:28]

It is clear that God created His people for His glory, for He speaks of His sons and daughters as those *who I created for my glory, who I formed and made."* [Isaiah 43:7] But it is not only human beings that God created for His purpose. The entire creation is intended to show God's glory. Even the inanimate creation - the stars and sun and moon and sky, testify to God's greatness:

> *"The heavens declare the glory of God; and the firmament shows His handiwork. Day by day utters speech and night unto night reveals*

knowledge."

The songs of heavenly worship in Revelation 4 connect God's creation of all things with the fact that He is worthy to receive glory from them.[1]

However, the first man, Adam, faced the first giant. Satan or the Serpent was the giant he had to face to pass the test of obedience to God. Adam and Eve lacked the knowledge to realise that Satan brought this temptation to them in order for him to destroy God's image in them.

God allows things to happen but not necessarily with His approval. God allows things to happen in our lives especially when it's our choice. For example, God allowed Samson to go ahead and marry a Philistine wife when it was against God's instruction to intermarry with Gentiles. Whatever choices God allows but does not approve of, can attract His wrath and judgement.

God allowed Eve and Adam to touch and eat the forbidden fruit in order to show Adam's level of obedience and commitment to God's instructions. The law of free will applies in this respect for man to choose between God's commandments and his desires. We believe that God is Omnipotent, Omniscient and Omnipresent. Therefore, God was aware that they had touched the forbidden fruit before He came to ask Adam where he was

1   *Wayne Grudem, Systematic Theology, page 271*

- proof that they could not hide themselves from God.

Could God prevent the touching of the fruit? Absolutely yes! But He decided to let Adam have his choice fulfilled. Hence, the pronouncement of God's verdict and the promise of restoration to man who had erred from the commandment of God.

The judgement of God was instant and had long-term effects. *"In all aspects of our lives"* Wayne Grudem writes *"It is amazing to see the extent to which Scriptures affirm that God brings about various events in our lives. For example, our dependence on God to give us food each day is affirmed every time we pray, 'Give us this day our daily bread.'* [Matthew 6:11] *Even though we work for our food and as far as mere human observation can discern, obtain it through entirely 'natural' causes. Similarly, Paul, looking at events with the eye of faith, affirms that 'my God will supply every need' of His children,* [Philippians 4:19] *even though God may use 'ordinary' means such as other people to do so."*[1]

Human beings, unlike God, usually give verdicts based on circumstantial evidence, and the opinions of witnesses, for example in the case of Jesus and Barrabas. This is the reason why we often see a verdict being challenged and the evidence found to be inadequate for one reason or the other.

---

1 Wayne Grudem, Systematic Theology, page 320

God sees into the future since He determines the end from the beginning. [Isaiah 46:10] He is the God of yesterday, today and tomorrow.

We all need to commit our lives to God since He can manage them better. God was rational in His judgement against Adam and Eve as well as the Serpent which had implications for the whole of creation.

God provides solutions to human problems. Remember that the wants of man are always insatiable or unquenchable and God is focused on meeting our needs, not our wants. Paul said - *"God shall supply all your need according to His riches in glory by Christ Jesus."* [Philippians 4:19]

Beware of the Serpent

The Bible says:

> *"God, who at various times and in various ways spoke in the time past to the fathers by the prophets, has in these last days spoken to us by His Son, whom He has appointed heir of all things, through whom He made the worlds"*
>
> [Hebrews 1:1-2]

We should be sensitive to the voice of God by the Holy Spirit to make the right decision in our lives in order to fight the giants in our lives.

The solution that God prescribed in Genesis

"the seed of the woman" [Genesis 3:15] was dispensed and perfected by Himself through the revealed Word of God - Jesus Christ, who is God that:

> *"Became flesh and dwelt among men and we behold his glory as the glory of the only begotten Son of the Father full of grace and truth."*
>
> [John 1:14]

In other words Jesus came to this world to die for mankind and free all from the curse of disobedience.

There will always be a giant and where there is a giant there will be a David to challenge the giant, and the God of Israel who gave David victory, will also give you victory over your giant. If you can recognise that giant, and call upon the Lord in prayer you can and rely on Him for your uncommon and supernatural victory.

You must have a renewed mind to discern God's revelation for the strategic method of dealing with your giants just as David did not struggle with his giant but approached him by faith and trust in the Word of the God of Israel. Like David, you have the capacity to receive divine help and support to overthrow your giant. It requires faith, confidence and application in the Word of God.

You cannot struggle with your giants and overcome them by your physical or mental powers alone, you will need spiritual weapons. [2 Corinthians 10:4] You need to acknowledge and accept the victory that has been given to you by God through the Lamb of God, Jesus Christ, who was slain on the cross for the salvation of the world.

The Purpose of Creating the First Man

The first man was created to have a relationship with his Creator. In this relationship lay the power of dominion given to him to exercise over all the other creatures that God created.

The Creator was not without proper organisation: Jehovah God is a God of order; He put things in place to make life easy for Adam, like a great organisation with a highly-skilled entrepreneur who put things in place for the smooth running of the business.

Jehovah created the man with a great purpose in mind. God is a God of purpose. Adam was created to work and not to stay idle; hence He made him a living soul, rational and creative.

Adam was created to be in charge of the garden, the business place of God. There were great resources in the garden to equip the man who was employed to do what God wanted him to do. Jesus said:

> *"The field is the world; the good seed are the children of the kingdom; but the tares are the children of the wicked*

ones."

The Lord Jesus Christ said the good seed and the tares should be left to grow together until the time of the harvest - His second coming.

These were the job specifications for Adam in the Garden of Eden:

- To dress the garden and keep it.

- To freely eat the fruit from the tree of the garden.

- To know the difference between the Tree of the knowledge of good and evil and other trees.

- To keep the Law that formed the basis of life in the Garden of Eden.

- To be responsible to God's commandments and instructions in the Garden of Eden.

The all-knowing God did all things perfectly so that Adam would not have any alibi in support of the wrong he may do. When Adam tried to shift the blame on to Eve, God immediately rejected his plea of mitigation for the offence he had committed.

Adam may have had just cause to accuse God if He had not given him free will to choose between obedience and disobedience.

It would be dishonourable of any employer to condemn his employee if he has not given him a job specification. Doing the job 'any how you like' is not know-how because know-how is specific and methodical.

God has a standard and He will not compromise, but it must be fully met. Without a standard, it would be impossible to achieve the desired goal, and a goal achieved yields a legacy for our posterity.

Giving guidelines His way of simplifying the pathway to our goals and showing us how to achieve them. There must be rapport between the employer and the employee. These were evident in the relationship between Adam and God before Adam 'blew it'. This must extend from the superior to the subordinate, creating room for feedback and allowing for variances and correction.

God came on a regular basis to see Adam to see how he was doing in the task given to him.

How many employers are only there as the boss whose interest is only in the financial and material gain? How many leaders in the Kingdom say something from the pulpit but act differently behind closed doors?

We should learn from God if we want to tackle and demolish giants and their strategies.

God is good; in fact, God was so good to

Adam that He created him as an active, rational being rather than a robot. Similarly, God wants you to function and flourish and be fruitful. His plan for you is absolutely marvellous with an expected end.

Therefore you must serve God in order to enjoy a good life and touch the lives of others; this is the most remarkable plan of God.

You must understand the basic reason for your existence on earth. God wants you to achieve the purpose for which He created you. He carefully made you for wonderful works so that He would be glorified in your existence. [Psalm 139:14]

God's Way

Despite God's ultimate plan for man, we still find it difficult to appreciate the goodness, plan and purpose of God. Man fell into the hands of the giant [Serpent] who twisted the truth and made it seem as robust as the truth when he was lying in a cunning and crafty way.

God did not condemn man but the Serpent and his action to do contrary to God's instructions. God exiled Adam from the Garden of Eden barring the way back so that a worse calamity would not befall mankind.

Jesus came to clear the debris of Satan and bruise his head to complete the task on the Cross of Calvary after which He said *"it is finished."* [Genesis 3:15; John 19:30]

The giants of your life can be tackled and defeated for your total victory. I pray that every giant chasing you will be demolished and your freedom will be immediate, in Jesus name, Amen.

The First Giant Emerged

> *"Now the Serpent was more cunning than any beast of the field which the Lord God had made. And he said to the woman, has God said you shall not eat of every tree of the garden?"*
> [Genesis 3:1]

There was an indication that Eve was not aware of what Satan was trying to do. Satan goes around with the purpose of causing destruction and he embarks on many strategies – deception being his greatest weapon:

> *"Satan is the father of lies. Jesus said, 'You are of your father the devil,and the desires of your father you want to do. He was a murderer from the beginning, and does not stand in the truth, because there is no truth in him. When he speaks a lie, he speaks from his own resources, for he is a liar and the father of it.'"*
> [John 8: 44]

God created all things perfectly but Satan fabricates lies in a subtle manner to distort the truth and make it look like the truth.

A distorted truth is as bad as 'contaminated milk' which is not good for any purpose. Eve could not realise that Satan was speaking lies to destroy and distort generations and the posterity of the human race.

Eve could have overcome the Serpent if she first identified who Satan was, where he came from, what he was after and what he wanted to achieve.

Beware of the Serpent in your life, marriage, home, 'in the street', in the Country and in your Church. He turns up in different colours, shapes and specifications every day as the technology is advancing.

There are those who look promising by their words and attitude as they appear intelligent, but the image of God is lacking in them.

There are many of them in the Churches today - they claim to know everything but lack the spiritual substance to activate the right things and the right thinking of God. They have nothing to lose or to gain but to destroy all things.

Satan actually tried to destroy the fabric of the purpose and plans of God for humanity. But the restoration will be completed and perfected in Jesus Christ who came to restore what the devil had destroyed.

It took Jesus three years of hard work going about doing good, and healing all that were oppressed by the devil. The first Adam failed the test of the giant; but the second Adam [Christ] defeated the giant and passed the test triumphantly. We can only triumph through Jesus Christ, the second and triumphant Adam. [1 Corinthians 15:21-22]

All giants will overpower you if you are not fully prepared for them. Jesus was fully and readily equipped for his own giants. Satan came the same way he came to the first Adam to tempt Jesus in a cunning way:

"Now when the tempter came to Him, he said, 'If You are the Son of God, command that these stones become bread.'"

[Matthew 4:3]

Satan tempted Adam and Eve with pride and envy, gluttony, and lust. Satan tried to repeat the same with Jesus but met with total failure. He failed because he could not successfully tempt the One who created him.

Jesus gave food to the hungry through the divine multiplication of the five loaves of bread and two small fishes. God the Father daily provided manna from heaven to His people in the wilderness. God will not tempt anyone neither can anyone ever succeed in tempting Him. [James 1:13]

We should therefore note the purpose of our creation, by understanding that there are giants ready to cunningly prevent us from fulfilling the our purpose. Choose the best approach to fight the fight of victory to conquer your giants. Use the wisdom of God His Word, through the power of Holy Spirit. Take the advice of those who have gone through similar experiences and have come out victorious. Do not give up the fight against your giants because you will surely win.

Chapter 2

The Meaning of Giants

What are Giants?

This chapter will describe from the Bible what the giants really look like and how to identify them in your life, and how to deal with them.

Firstly, giants in this context are substances, persons, things, and spirits that can come your way to prevent you from achieving your divine assignment, and sabotage your creative blessings, joy, destiny, God-given life ambitions as well as your God-given promises.

Giants are giants if we regard them as giants. We should refrain from promoting hindrances to our destiny as giants are like trees that God did not plant which can be uprooted from our lives. We should therefore face our giants head on to achieve victory that lasts.

From every chapter of the Bible, you can see one or more giants. They are intimidating in various forms - destiny killers, blessing robbers, and ambition destroyers. They look like clouds and you should therefore remember that clouds will never stay long or last forever; they will soon dissipate and the light will shine again.

Genesis 3 reveals the high tempo of deceit

by Satan to lure man into doing what was contrary to the command of God. Satan came in a way man could never have imagined. What Satan was doing was to rob man of his right and power which God accorded him in the first place at creation:

"Now the serpent was more cunning than any beast of the field which the Lord God had made. And he said to the woman - 'Has God indeed said, you shall not eat of every tree of the garden?'"

[Genesis 3:1]

This he did to exploit man's limited understanding of God's commandments.

Every giant may not necessarily come in an arrogant way and brag as in the case of David and Goliath. They all manifest through some form of trickery and craftiness to gain entry into your life to manipulate you.

Abram and Sarai faced the giant of barrenness which led to their impatient decision to have a son with Hagar, her handmaiden, who bore Abram his first son Ishmael, but he was not God's 'child of promise'. This was the promise of God for Abraham but the giant of hopelessness, impatience and wrong decisions led Abram to attempt to help God to fulfil His promise.

The impatience of Abram led to the perpetual rift among his descendants, Ishmael and Isaac who later became the Palestinians and the Jews and whose conflict remains unsettled to this day. Though Abram was given unconditional promises, his impatience have become a lesson for all generations. Faith is not faith if it has not confronted and conquered the giants of doubt, impatience and hopelessness. How often do you forfeit your God-given promise and destiny because of your refusal to wait and see the plan, purpose and glory of God for your life?

Points to Note

- The promise of God may tarry or delay yet it still remains intact and it will surely come to pass at God's appointed time. The appointed time is the time God wants His promises for your life to come into fulfilment. The appointed time is the time of God and His time is always the best for you. [Habakkuk 2:3]

- There may be clouds over the promises and it may look as if it is not possible for them to be fulfilled, yet you must believe that God will clear the clouds for the promises to be fulfilled. Therefore, you must wait prayerfully and patiently for God's promises for your life.

- You must believe God in all your ways and that He can never lie even when if seems that God has forgotten you. Scripture says:

*"God is not a man that He should
lie; neither the son of man that
He should repent: hath He said,
and shall He not do it? Or hath He
spoken, and shall He not make it
good"*

[Numbers 23:19 KJV]

God will never forget you as He has
promised. [Isaiah 49:15]

- Whenever God makes a promise
  and you are at the crossroads of the
  promise with a daunting task ahead
  of you, you must believe that God
  who made the promise for you is
  with you in that trouble. He will lead
  you through the turbulent time to
  achieve the promise He has made for
  you. God will make you a winner and
  not a loser. God is aware of all the
  problems that will overtake you in life
  and how you can escape them or go
  through and come out as a winner.

- God is behind your success and any
  obstruction that comes your way will
  be removed by Him. God prophesied
  about the slavery of the children of
  Israel and how He was going to bring
  them out of the tribulation of slavery.
  [Genesis15:13-21]

- The giants whom the Israelites
  met in Egypt appeared unbeatable,
  presenting themselves to the people

as gods.

- God gave Pharaoh and the Egyptians
  time to perform and finish all they
  could do before God came down
  on them in a heavy-handed way,
  He afflicted the Egyptians with ten
  plagues [Exodus 7-11]:

  In the first plague God turned the
  waters to blood and so made them
  undrinkable.

  The second plague unleashed frogs
  on the territory of the Egyptians.

  The third plague was lice which
  God used to cover the whole land
  of Egypt.

  The fourth plague was flies. God
  sent swarms of flies on the land to
  terrify them.

  The fifth plague was livestock
  disease.

  The sixth plague was boils with
  which God afflicted man and beast
  throughout the land of Egypt.

  The seventh plague was hail. God
  caused heavy hail to rain down
  throughout their land.

  The eighth plague were locusts
  that bombarded the land of Egypt
  to destroy their crops.

The ninth plague was darkness. There was thick darkness in all the land of Egypt for three days.

The tenth and final plague was the death of all first-born of men and beasts.

- When Christians and giants engage in battle, giants cannot and will never win if they have submitted themselves to God. God is always present to help in time of trouble and He is your *"refuge and strength."* [Psalm 46:1] You should not be moved by your troubles because God is with you. God will speak and your mountain will melt.

- Giants can never knock you out with their temporary applause unless you knock yourself out with your unbelieving mind. God is waiting, and watching your giants and He has His own strategy for defeating them. There is a time for God to fight the battle of your life. Before God steps into the ring on your behalf, He has already given you victory. [Exodus 2:23-25]

- God will surely deliver you if you call on Him with a prayer of faith. He will acknowledge you if you wait on Him for your deliverance.

- God brought about the exodus of the

Israelites, but Egypt still remained a threat to them because it was recalled in their dreams, thoughts, reasoning, and imaginations. Similarly, if you dwell in your past and refuse to let go of the 'Egypt' you have left behind, you will remain in bondage to your past giants.

- God had ordained the Promised Land for the Israelites, but they refused to acknowledge His faithfulness to the promise He had made. Their focus was on the giants. They should have seen the land as having been reserved for them by Jehovah who owns the heavens and earth. [Psalm 24:1]

- God and his promises to His people are greater than any opposition from giants that arise along your way.

- The inability to trust God prevented them from rising above their fearful imaginations.

- Although the giants were not as daunting as the ones God conquered for them in the past, they struggled to trust that what God had done in the past He would do again.

- They lifted up the giants and relegated their God who has dominion over all creatures. They branding themselves as grasshoppers in the sight of their 'defeated' giants. [Numbers 13:32-33]

- All giants you face are defeated. You should celebrate their defeat and never think about them in the realm of your spirit. Every child of God should trust he has received victory over the giants - whatever shape or imagination they may take.

- The Israelites went to spy out the Promised Land and they confirmed it to be flowing with milk and honey but failed to claim the substance they had seen as theirs. [Numbers 13:1-3] God had a good intention for their spying. They were to survey the Land that they were about to possess as their inheritance.

- Their visit to the Promised Land was not for negative comment but for confirming their ownership of the land. All they needed to do was to come back with the report of what they had seen with the assurance of faith that what God had promised, He was able to deliver. Never look at the obstacle to your God-given inheritance, but rather look unto God and the Promise He has made for you.

- We are all coming out from the land of slavery whether it be spiritual or physical slavery. The Land of Promise is loaded with blessing, satisfaction and contentment. If we believe Jesus, we shall see that in Jesus the promise is fulfilled.

- Many Children of God have already settled for defeat before the fight against their giants has even started. The Israelites settled for defeat in the midst of victory assured by God. [Numbers 13:32-33] They were prophesying negativity into their lives and refusing to claim the victory that God had planned for them.

- Never forget that the thought of God for you is a thought of goodness and an expected end. [Jeremiah 29:11, Proverbs 23:7] The promise is just for you. And God is too big to make a promise without ensuring it is fulfilled. Therefore God will make good on His promise to His children. [Hebrew 6:18]

- God will always prove you wrong if you doubt Him. His promises are as good as He who made the promise. Whenever you have the promise of God, you should be ready and expecting the fulfilment of such a promise at the appointed time.

How to claim God's promises

Whenever God promises us something, we should not exaggerate the obstacles that are in our way and think that those obstacles will hinder God's promises from fulfilment. Some of the Israelites were united in their unbelief and came up with negative reports which were greatly exaggerated with the effect of enhancing their unbelief and demeaning the power and presence of God with them. They turned the Promised Land and their giants into something evil, intimidating and unconquerable. Hence their contemptuous description [Number 13:32] was ultimately an attack on God who was the giver of the Promised Land.

Points to note

- God will not tolerate any scandalous language from people, whatever reasons or excuses they may give to justify negative thoughts about God and His promises.

- You should trust God for His promises despite what people may think or say against you because of the promise.

- You should think, see and act the way God thinks, sees and acts.

- You should always use the Word of God and His promises to encourage yourself to counteract any negative thoughts that may arise in your heart.

- Never follow the multitude to do evil even when they are in the majority. You should always remember and understand that it is true that even one with God is a majority. In fact, God on His own is the majority since God will require no help to carry out His purpose. [Exodus 23:2]

- Let all the words that proceed out of your mouth lead you to receive the promise of God for your life. Use the power of your tongue wisely to lead you to God's planned goal or destiny for you. [Proverbs 18:21; Colossians 3:15-16]

God's Judgement on the rebels

God pronounced a death sentence on the rebels. [Numbers 14:26-29] God can use any means or method to defend your cause. Rebelling against God and His people or His ministers is dangerous and can lead to serious consequences. [Psalm 105:15] God defended Moses from the hands of Korah, Dathan and Abiram's rebellion. Rebelling against ministers of God is the same as rebelling against God which can incur dangerous consequences. You must always take your leave from people who want to rebel against the children of God and the ministers of God. Korah, Dathan and Abiram in their wicked solidarity with others, received their punishment from God along with their families. [Numbers 16:11-32]

The Wall of Jericho as a Giant

The wall of Jericho was one of the greatest obstacles which the Israelites faced having crossed over to the Promise Land. [Joshua 6:1-2] Before claiming and receiving the promises of God for your life, you are bound to face a similar wall of discouragement that looks like an obstruction to the hidden treasures that God has prepared for you. The following are some points to note before you can surmount the seemingly insurmountable walls of Jericho in your life:

Points to Note

- Identify the wall of Jericho before you and know for sure that it will require the assistance of the One who is greater than you, to pull it down.

- Listen attentively to God's instructions directly or through God's appointed servants for the divine explanations, directions and guidance.

- Allow God to speak concerning your wall of Jericho.

- Ignore the environmental and climatic factors that may blind you to seeing and knowing the greatness of

God's power and presence.

- Be encouraged even when your Jericho-like situation is proving stubborn.

- Speak to God constantly regarding the issues at stake.

- Confess God's revelation about your situation.

- We should strongly believe in God who is the only One who has the solution to all problems and is surely not a God of confusion.

- Believe that every wall of Jericho in your life has fallen no matter how intimidating they may seem; but God will allow it to be there to show His divine power over all nature. This can be the case after you have prayed over a situation that looks stubborn and are beginning to think it can never be conquered despite the assurance both from the Word of God and God directly speaking to your spirit.

- Be ready to shout for joy in the midst of tribulation and intimidation and claim the joy of the Lord as your strength. [Joshua 6:20-21; Nehemiah 8:10]

- Shouting for joy when you are in the

midst of trouble is a sign of walking in faith and trusting the Lord that there can be no weapon formed against your life that can prosper. [Isaiah 54:17]

Naomi's Experience with a Giant

The Book of Ruth revealed another example of a giant which nearly wiped away the whole family or the posterity of Elimelech. [Ruth 1:1-4] Elimelech forgot that God is Jehovah Jireh who meets our need in the midst of difficult times or seasons. [Genesis 22:12-14; Nehemiah 8:10]

The situation that led Naomi and Elimelech to a foreign land - Moab was forbidden by God for the children of Israel - is a great lesson to all who want to understand and enjoy the goodness of God.

They lost everything. Naomi eventually re-gained much through the God of Israel whom Ruth, the Moabite woman, believed and devotedly trusted to follow for the rest of her life.

God always proves Himself faithful regardless of opposition we may face, He always performs His part of any covenant for His people.

The return of Naomi and Ruth

Though Naomi and Ruth returned to Bethlehem in misery, the God of miracles who brings something out of nothing was waiting and also leading them to His desired destiny. Hence, they failed to realise that the plan of God was abundantly following them to reveal Him the true God who can be trusted.

Points to note

- It is never too late to come back to God who is waiting for you to make a u-turn and re-unite with Him. [Luke 15:20-22]

- Humble yourself under the arm of God who can deliver you from the hands of your opponents and oppressors. [Hebrews 12:12-13]

- Be consistent with what you believe about God. [Colossians 2:6]

- Associate with the right men and women of principle. [Proverbs 13:20]

- There is divine favour for those who endure to the end. [Matthew 24:13]

- Those who endure to the end shall be saved. [Matthew 24:13; Isaiah 40:31]

David's experience of a Giant

The story of David and Goliath has been a focal point in all Christian gatherings because of the way the story fits in into all facets of human struggles. It teaches us how every 'Child of God' can conquer their giants against all odds through total reliance on God. After God had rejected Saul as king of Israel, the Lord commanded Samuel to go and anoint David as king over Israel. [1 Samuel 16:1] David was the choice of God to be King over Israel. The choice of God is never based on experience, qualification, or on hierarchical position but on divine disposition and appointment.

Goliath had just the right credentials for anyone to hire him for military service. While David was an amateur, Goliath was a professional mercenary of a reputable record. David was a very godly, ruddy lad who took care of his father's flock. Though forgotten by his dad in the day Samuel came, God took his matter up beyond what a man will forget and anointed the right person to be the king. God chose David to confound the mighty army of the Philistines under the command of Goliath.

Goliath was great in the sight of the Philistines and they believed that through him the battle against the Israelites would be won. Goliath was like an ant in the sight of Jehovah, the Lord of hosts, who fights and always wins the battle.

You should always trust that - *"the weapons of [your] warfare are not carnal but mighty in God for pulling down strongholds."* [2 Corinthians 10:4]

Therefore, always use your weapons of prayer and spiritual power to pray to God who answers prayers.

David's past victories over a lion and a bear gave him the faith to trust God for subsequent victory over Goliath. David retrospectively thanked and trusted God for his victory.

The battle of David and Goliath was more of a theological crisis, it was the Israelites' lack of faith rather than any military inadequacy that was the issue. What David lacked in military experience or age he more than up for in his faith in God to give him victory over Goliath God was bound by his covenant to curse Goliath. [Genesis 12:3]

David, as small as he was, depended on the power of God as the warrior and defender of His people. [Exodus 15:3] David was physically small but spiritually big and dangerous to Goliath who was ignorant of the God of Israel's winning power.

Points to note

- We must have at the back of our minds that our expected victory must be demonstrated to the world so that they will know that the God of Israel is alive forever and governs every situation in our lives.

- God delivers His own people against overwhelming odds. David put the contest with his giant into the proper perspective by saying that *"the battle is the Lord's."* [1 Samuel 17:47]

- David did not regard Goliath as a giant, [1 Samuel 17: 26-31] but as an uncircumcised Philistine.

- David's faith in the God of Israel who delivers never shakes even in the face of the well-credited local champion, Goliath.

- David relied on the God of Hosts which means that God is the Commander-in-Chief of the armies of heaven and of His people.

- David was driven by a divine strategy which no man should underestimate. Hence his stone was guided by the Lord to Goliath's forehead, and thus the Philistine was defeated.

- The enemy of your life, 'your giant', must be totally eliminated, when David struck Goliath he also defeated the Philistine army. Then the head of Goliath was cut off and brought to King Saul as a testimonial.

- David pursued the Philistines to a point of no return where they became powerless, northward to Ekron and eastward to Gath. [1 Samuel 17:51-52]

It took David just one day to defeat Goliath who had been bragging to the Israelites for forty days without any one daring to confront him. Similarly, if you believe and trust the Lord, the giants that have been chasing you for years can be destroyed within twenty four hours or just in the 'nick of time'.

David came back from the battlefield, to face the personal warfare between himself and Saul. Though victory and success may attract many people to you, not everyone who joins in celebrating your success, may be sincere.

David deserved to be commended for the victory, by God's power. Instead he received an unexpected and brutal backlash. Saul began to resent David because of the adulation he received from the people, and this led to his decision to end the life of David by any means. [1 Samuel 18:8-11]

It took David one day to conquer Goliath who had been a threat to the people of Israel for a long time; but it was many years before David became king, during which he had many opportunities to slay Saul but did not do so for fear of harming God's anointed king.

We all have to fight battles with friends and family at some time, and they are always difficult to overcome. The enemy within is a most dangerous thing to tackle in life, such giants whilst appearing outwardly friendly, may indeed be 'wolves in sheep's clothing'.

Points to note

- David fought his giants and won through the support of God; he called it 'the battle of the Lord of Hosts'.

- David humbled himself because of the confidence he had in God which led to victory.

- David's case study is similar to what is happening in the church around the world today. We must make sure that every Goliath in the Church of God is defeated. Trees that we did not plant, and whose existence is undesirable, must be cut off and uprooted completely and replaced with good trees.

- Though Saul tried to put his armour on David it did not fit him. This is because God had already armed David for victory. Hence the armour of Saul was not fit for purpose.

- Goliath mocked and ridiculed David not seeing or knowing that he had the best military garrison - the heavenly host of God with him.

- David was small but the invisible armies of God were with him ready to fight on his behalf. David was doing the talking while Jehovah was doing the fighting. [2 Kings 6:16, 1 John

4:4] You must speak the Word of God to your giants.

- Do not fight evil with evil, [Romans 12:17] just as David lived peacefully with king Saul his enemy. [Romans 12:18; Proverb 16:7; Hebrews 12:14]

- God fought the extended battle with Saul and brought David to the throne He had promised him. *"Weeping may endure for a night, but joy comes in the morning."* [Psalm 30:5] Your night - evil days - may be days, weeks, even years; but joy comes when you break free from your struggles.

- David kept the secret of the Lord within him [Psalm 25:14] since he knew the promise of God - the throne of Israel - would not fail. He dared not allow the temporary pain of Saul's persecution to derail his destiny.

- The best way to fulfil your destiny is to walk in the wisdom and strategy of God.

- Do not be in a hurry; do not be afraid, do not be dismayed because of the giants around you. The invisible God who has power to deal with all your giants is with you.

- He is the invisible, invincible God. He is greater and more powerful than the giants around that you can see or feel. [2 Kings 6:16; 1 John 4:4]

- David would only listen to God's voice - Saul wanted him to put on his armour, to be equipped like Goliath but David refused knowing he had been empowered by the Lord even before Saul brought him armour that did not fit.

- There was no support for David before he fought Goliath, his brothers were vehemently against him. [1 Samuel 17:28] Even if your family and friends forsake you, the Lord will fight for you. [Psalm 27:10] Saul doubted David's integrity and ability to face Goliath, but David knew he would have God's abilities. You too have the capacity to confront and defeat your giants.

- David had the backing of the Lord and so there was no need for him to fear, together they formed the majority he needed to win against the forces of the enemies of the people of God.

- David had no doubt in his heart that he could defeat Goliath in God's strength. The confidence and faith David had built up over time was strong. Do not let yourself down - heaven is behind anyone that fully trusts in the name of the Lord. [1 John

3:20-22; Isaiah 28:16]

- David sought the grace of God - nothing else can help you to fight the fight of faith and win. There is no big or small grace just the grace of God which is sufficient for you. It's not only unmerited favour but it is the Power of God and the finished work of Jesus on the cross. [2 Peter 1:2-3]

- David choose five smooth stones from the brook but he only used one to defeat the arrogant Goliath. [1Samuel 17:40]

- The word G R A C E has five letters and the five stones might be considered symbolic of the glorious mercy and grace of God that David received. Out of the grace of God comes victory for you. God told Apostle Paul - *"My grace is sufficient for you."* [2 Corinthians 12:9]

- It was the Lord on David's side that granted him victory over the proud Goliath. Grace is always sufficient to meet your challenges whatever form they may take.

- You may be weak or powerless but with reliance on the grace of God, victory is guaranteed.

- God always wins battles by empowering His faithful servants.

David only used one stone out of the five he picked up. If David used all five stones, it would still have been the grace of God that won the fight. The grace of God paves the way for the victory you need and such victory has no limit.

- You need the grace of God in your life and ministry to be victorious and successful. It is good to pray for the grace of God at all times.

- David was equipped with the invisible weapons and gadgets of the God; king Saul was trying to put on David the physical armour but he refused because God had already put on him His own armour. Your spiritual weapons to defeat your giants are not carnal but mighty in the Lord to pull down their strongholds. [2 Corinthians 10:4]

- A 'child of God' does not need any additional armour of the flesh. You are already equipped by the invisible armour of God so you need not try any other armour.

- David was equipped to fight the Philistine armies; God's battle is won before the start, and David fought as God led him.

- When God leads and directs your affairs, the deal is done. Remember the battle is of the Lord, get ready to heed God's instructions. [2 Chronicles 20:15]

The instructions of God are to help you and lead the way to your victory. Where He leads you, you must go. Whereas man's way may lead to personal gain and benefits, God's way results in His name being glorified.

Chapter 3

How to Identify Your Giants

Giants appear in different forms, shapes, and sizes. What is a giant to Mr. A may not be a giant to Mr. B. What may have been a giant to Joseph may not have been considered a giant to Nehemiah. Goliath was by no means the only giant. Giants can also manifest spiritually and physically, as well as through imaginations and thoughts.

Giants are not giants until you refer to or recognise them as such. Weapons can be formed but that does not necessarily mean they will prosper over you. You have an advocate and defender who intercedes for and defends you at all times. [1 John 2:1]

Jesus has won the battle in your life you thought was impossible to won. We should therefore worry less about the battles which have been won by Jesus on at cross at Calvary.

Giants can be physical as was the case with Goliath. [1 Samuel 17] Goliath showed himself as a giant against David and the Israelite army, but David only saw him as an *"uncircumcised Philistine"*.

David knew the secret of the Lord - that the battle is not truly fought with physical weapons, but rather through faith in God and the confession of His Word.

Who ever applies the secret of the Lord will know how to fight and overcome any giant. Who then a winner? A winner may appear defeated at the beginning but will celebrat God's victory over all his adversaries in the end.

With God fighting your battle, you can go through situations that seem overwhelming and impossible to overcome. You will have the last laugh!

Do not lose your faith and your hope; fix your hope on Jesus who is your anchor. He will take you from start to finish with victory assured. [Hebrew 10:35 & 12:1-2]

The fall of the righteous has no destructive effect on their progress in life. It only slows them down a bit to change them into better and progressive achievers. Remember that the righteous may fall seven times but they will rise again. [Proverbs 24:16]

The giants use many ways and approaches to gain access into your life, including through your wife, husband, friend, a gift, an imagination as well as thoughts. There are many who behave like friends but their hearts are full of poisons that can easily destroy your life.

Your thoughts at times become giants and prevent you from moving to the next level of your life. The thoughts of your past failures, family failures, financial failures, sickness, and domestic problems can become your giants. You should remember that there is only one solution to all these giants. The revelation of the word of God is the answer. Jesus is the way to your breakthrough in every situation. Every demon is conquerable by the name of Jesus Christ. You don't "counsel" demons out of people; nor do demons come out when a person becomes more disciplined. Demons only come out by the power of Christ.

Whatever the Word of God did not establish concerning you is not part of what God has in store for you, and you should not claim it to be part of your life. No longer reflect on your past problems as they are stepping stones to great achievement.

Do not allow your past to dictate and direct your future. Jesus is the way forward, allow him to lead you. God is the owner of everything and Jesus is empowered to lead you and give you access to God and His plans and purposes for your life.

Giants are conquered through Jesus. He is the conqueror in all ages past. Those who wait on Him are super-conquerors. This is why you are made "more than a conqueror" [Romans 8:37] because Jesus loves you.

Do not allow your 'family giant' to conquer you before you face other battles you are about to defeat. Every believer is a potential winner. David's brothers and king Saul wanted him to stay behind and watch the

Philistines hero harassing the Israelites. [1 Samuel 17:28-29]

David rejected the fear his bothers were trying to create. He moved forward to win the battle. At first it seemed irrational to David's brothers to see him going forward to fight Goliath whom every Israelite feared as a mighty warrior. [1 Samuel 17:27-33]

The intimidating stance and fearful advice of David's brothers could not stop David's destiny to defeat Goliath with the aid of God's power. In the end Israel sang praises the praises of Almighty God.

Points to note

- Where there is no pain to overcome, there will be no gain to celebrate.

- You must see beyond your problems at hand to gain the power for your future role and responsibility.

- Never allow any circumstance to distract you from pursuing your God-given vision.

- Use your previous God-given victory as your testimonial to win another battle. [1 Samuel 17: 34-37]

- Always be bold and courageous for the task at hand, since God will always back those who step out in faith.

- David relied on the Lord for his victory over Goliath. Whenever you rely on God for help, He will inspire you to face your battle. [1 Samuel 17:37]

- Do not think that there is any battle to big for God to win, He is a triumphant God.

- Always arm yourself with the Word of God, a winning tool.

- Do not be moved by the presence of those things that present themselves as 'goliaths' or by any imagination, thought, or feeling concerning the past or future.

- Though Goliath appeared to be physically strong enough to defeat David, he lacked spiritual strength. David possessed the supernatural power of God which enabled him to win battles. Children of God must know and have what it takes to be winners the battles of life.

- You should remember that there is no success without resentment from the opposition. You must be ready to manage the forces of resistance on your way to victory and success.

Types of Giants

There is no greater giant than the one conquered by the Jesus Christ on the cross - the devil. Jesus actually combined together all visible and invisible giants at a go and destroyed them for the benefit of all who will receive Him as Lord and Saviour.

Ultimately there is only one giant called Satan. He has many fallen associates who have different missions against humanity. They have tempted God's people with different problems, at different times and on different occasions.

Satan is the architect of all human problems. Jesus is aware of this and he said - *"For this purpose the Son of God was manifested that He might destroyed the works of the devil."* [1 John 3:8]

It was on the cross that Jesus purchased freedom for mankind. The sinless Jesus carried the sin of humanity and made the atonement for the sins of all.

Satan and his angels still pose as giants and people see them as such, but he was conquered on the cross by Jesus Christ for you.

Never give him any attention. If you do so, he will try to direct your affairs. This is not to say that you should be ignorant of the devices of the enemy. Do not put yourself in bondage because of the fear of a giant. Trust

in God to give you the victory you need.
[Hebrew 2:15]

The giants that you recognise are defeated
giants. They are like plants inside the pot
that can be destroyed at any time. Though
they flourish, they are under your control
or the control of the Gardener [Father God];
they can only grow if you feed them with
nutrients; but you can inhibit their growth by
using the necessary strategies. Stop feeding
your giants with wrong motives, decisions,
lifestyles and aspirations.

Points to Note

- You have the authority to fight and
  defeat your giants which manifest
  through the works of the flesh such
  as drunkenness, jealousy, hatred,
  envy, theft, fornication. [Galatians
  5:19-21] These are the things we all
  too often try to overcome with by
  our own strength, but are unable to
  defeat.

- Adam received God's authority
  and power to defeat and dominate
  Satan but he willingly gave away
  this authority to Satan. Jesus, the
  last Adam, came to reclaim this
  authority and power and give it
  back to humanity without which no
  man would ever be able to exercise
  victory over Satan and sin.

- Satan came to tempt Jesus in the

same cunning way he did in the Garden of Eden, to deceive Eve and caused Adam to sin, but Jesus defeated him by the Word of God.

- Jesus now holds the title deeds of all power in heaven and on earth and promised to hand over the power to whoever believes in Him so that they can exercise the same power by faith. [John 1:11-12]

- In David's time, the giant came in the form of Goliath, that was physical; but in these latter days giants can come in more sophisticated ways. Now that we are living in the age of technology, Satan uses the all forms of media to try to ensnare our minds.

- Technology can be used for good or evil, it is a useful tool for the children of God. You can use technology to glorify God and have a wonderful life that He has promised you or use it to glorify Satan and live a defeated and frustrated life.

- Technology must be used rightly to glorify God. [Exodus 31:1-7] If technology is rightly used, it will bring glory to God and joy and satisfaction into our lives.

- Do not give the giant any attention or foothold to direct your affairs.

- You have the authority of God in your life and you must exercise it as Jesus did against Satan to defeat your giants.

- Believe in the power of God and His dominion over all Satan's schemes.

The Giant of 'Financial Poverty'

Poverty is a deadly disease as well as a curse to humanity. It is an inability to afford the means of exchange for what you need, either by having no money or other means of exchange to acquire what you need.

Recall the story of the widow of one of Elisha's prophets [2 Kings 4:1-7] Her husband had died and the creditor was coming with the intention of enslaving her two sons.

At this point she was probably unable to think straight. Her giant would have set fear and despondency into her mind, the creditor was in control. Her situation was like being dead without being buried.

God's intervention in the life of the widow meant that her life robustly changed for the better.

You should pray to God to deliver you from financial debt. It can lead to horrific situations but bear in mind that throughout the world many hold debt in the form of a mortgage which has become the norm. Debt can lead to horrific consequences when people fail to keep on top of their repayments. Jesus reminds us that all we need is food and clothing to maintain our daily lives. [Matthew 6:25-34]

You should not forget that God Himself gave man the power to get wealth so that He might establish His covenant which He swore to our fathers and which still applies to His children today. [Deuteronomy 8:18]

Financial prosperity is an endowment from God to meet all your needs. Even though human desires or wants can be insatiable at times, Hi promise is to meet our needs. Note there is a difference between 'need' and 'want'.

God is a covenant-fulfilling God and He wants you to achieve and have great fulfilment in order to demonstrate the marvellous love He has bestowed on you.

Jesus modelled the prayer - *"Give us this day our daily bread."* Poverty is a disaster to human life, it can cause those afflicted to pray for their lives to be cut short.

The Bible reveals that poverty during the siege of Samaria by the Syrians led to some people making arrangements for eating their children in rotation. [2 Kings 6:28-30]

Poverty coupled with greed, has led to some evil and devilish activities, destruction of lives and corruption in to many nations.

A poor man wants the world to come to an end today while the rich man wants it to continue so that he can accomplish his business objectives and enjoy his wealth.

Poverty must be prayed about and action taken to erase and wipe it out from our lives and society so that we may live the number of our days on earth in full, with blessing and good health by the grace of God.

Why not go back to God and ask Him to bless you, enlarge your territory, and keep you from the pain of poverty. We should all cry out to God like Jabez so that our lives will also be changed. God intervened in his life and blessed him after he had prayed. The prayer of Jabez became famous among Christians all over the world because of the fruitful result of his prayer. [1 Chronicles 4:9-10]

You need to go before the throne of mercy in prayer and have your life changed by God. If you do, your life will become an example for other people to emulate. However, your vision must be backed up by action that will cause you to achieve the God-given purpose for your life. Think right and follow the right direction.

Points to note

- It is good to pray for the blessings that will change your life and character into the true image of God.

- It is good to experience the blessings

that will serve you and others. Resist becoming a slave to money or the riches that God has given to you for good.

- It is good to be a blessing to many lives in the church and around the world.

In the Lion's Den

It is easy to pose as strong if you have never experienced difficulties or problems. The psalmist declared - *"It is good for me that I have been afflicted that I might learn thy statutes."* [Psalm 119:71 KJV]

- In Daniel 6, we read about the death sentence passed on Daniel, a man of God, for his refusal to compromise his faith in the true God of Israel. Daniel was a pious and faithful man with an excellent spirit and God delivered him from the lion's den.

- A time of trial and weeping must surely come to the life of someone who is about to be lifted up by God. Blessing will follow your suffering and afflictions. Though many are the afflictions of the righteous, it is true that God will definitely deliver them from them all. [Psalms 34:19]

- There should be nothing on earth to deter you from serving Jehovah God, the Alpha and Omega. As the

Scripture declares:

"What then shall we say to these things? If God is for us, who can be against us?"

[Romans 8:31]

"Who shall separate us from the love of Christ? Shall tribulation, or distress, or persecution, or famine, or nakedness, or peril, or sword? "

[Romans 8:35]

At one time or the other in your life, you will be thrown into a 'lion's den' through false accusations or conspiracy and you will feel as if you have been forgotten there. But when everyone forgets you, the King of kings will not forget you. He will come to rescue you from the lion's den; as the Scripture declares - *"Weeping may endure for a night but joy comes in the morning."* [Psalm 30:5; Isaiah 49:15-17, Psalm 27:10, Daniel 6:19-22]

Remember that you are hated because of your star that has risen and is shining and will shine even more brightly. Joseph was hated because of his dream and his star that was about to shine. His rebellious brothers conspired to kill him and to deter him from achieving the vision which Jehovah had given him, but the dream came to pass in spite of them.

When Daniel was taken captive in Babylon, he had to leave all his possessions behind, but this did not change his loyalty towards

God. Daniel was fervent in prayer and devotion in the midst of tribulation; he did not deny the God of his fathers because of 'food for a season' and 'position for a minute'.

He knew that God would be dependable in times of joy as well as sorrow, whether there was economic boom or downturn. Daniel became one of the top officials in Babylon [Daniel 6:2] but did not allow the position to go to his head and destroy his hope in the God of Israel.

As a chief member of king Darius's cabinet, [Daniel 6:1-2] Daniel should have been the first to honour the command of the king and pray only to the king who had made himself god, but he would not do that:

> *"Now when Daniel knew that the writing was signed, he went home; and in his upper room, with his windows open toward Jerusalem, he knelt down on his knees three times that day and prayed and gave thanks before his God as was his custom since early days"*
>
> [Daniel 6:10]

Those who will stand for God must stand against all forms of idolatry.

The devil can conspire to convince you that you are not going to make it, because you have flouted the traditions of the land or you have failed to honour the 'ancestors' idols'. This could be intimidating but those who know the God they serve will be strong and do great exploits like Daniel. [Daniel 11:32]

Even if the whole world were to plot against the men and women of God who persistently stand on the Word of God, they will not fail nor fall.

When all is said and done, God fights for His people against every plot of the enemy; so let us stand by the standard of God and His Word. He will surely fight our battles and we will be winners. The Apostle Peter advises us:

"Let us therefore add to our faith virtue; and to virtue knowledge; and to knowledge temperance or self control; and self control patience and to patience godliness and to godliness brotherly kindness; and to brotherly kindness, love. For if this things be in you and abound we will neither be barren nor unfruitful in the knowledge of our Lord Jesus Christ."
[2 Peter 1:5-10]

Chapter 4

Overcoming Your Giants

How Giants Operate

Children of God must arm themselves with knowledge of the devices of Satan. [2 Corinthians 2:11] We should allow the Holy Spirit to lead and direct us in all the things we want to embark on at all times. Before we start something new, we should seek advice where necessary, from people who know more than we do so that we can succeed. This is because we need additional knowledge to be fruitful. [2 Peter 2:5-7]

Satan may not come in the form of a terrifying 'Goliath' but often comes in the form of things which appear beneficial. The operational methods of the enemy are vast and may be overlooked if care is not taken.

The giants can come in the form of a friends who claim to love you but who are really enemies. Run from them because they are wolves in sheep's clothing.

These 'giants' can come as a gift knocking at your door or as a 'free lunch'. Satan works through men and women to accomplish his task.

The schemes of Samballat and Tobiah could not stop Nehemiah in pursuing his objective of rebuilding the wall and gates of Jerusalem. [Nehemiah: 6:1-3]

Satan wants you to commit sin to snatch you to his side; as the Scripture declares:

"He who commits sin is of the devil for the Devil sins from the beginning, and for this purpose the Son of God manifested that he might destroy the work of the Devil."

[1 John 3:8]

However, we must always rely on the power of God's forgiveness as the Bible reassures us that:

"If we confess our sins, He is faithful and just to forgive us our sins and to cleanse us from all unrighteousness."

[1 John 1:9]

There are many 'schemes of Satan' in the lives of all children of God and they can manifest in the following ways:

- He can be permitted to afflict the righteous. [Job: 1:12]

- He claims authority over the world to do whatever he wants to do. [Luke 4:6]

- He blinds the minds of unbelievers. [2 Corinthians 4:3-4]

- He tempts people to disobey God. [Genesis 3: 1-4]

- He slandering the saints as in the life of Job. [Job 1:9-11]

- He travels to places to oppose the children of God. [Zechariah 3:1-4]
- He tempts human beings to sin against God. [John 13:2]

Satan is preying on men and women all the time but nevertheless we have the duty of resisting him and submitting ourselves to God; we are re-assured that if we resist the devil, he will flee from us. [1 Peter 5:8-9; Ephesians 4:26-27; James 4:7-8]

In addition you must put on the whole armour of God [Ephesians 6:11] that you may be able to stand against the wiles of the devil [giants]. Let the Word of God control all your actions. You may be persecuted but rest assured that you will have the last laugh.

The Conqueror of Giants

Christ went to the cross to fight the giant and won the battle by his blood. Jesus handed down the winning prize of being a conqueror to all children of God who are co-heirs to the Kingdom of His Father. You have received the special favour of God to operate in the light of what Jesus Christ has achieved for you. You are more than a conqueror through Jesus. This implies that you received the special favour and victory of Jesus without going to the battlefield to fight for them.

Satan fears the Name given to Jesus

because of His victory on the Cross. The Bible confirmed this as follows:

> *"Therefore God also has highly exalted Him and given Him the Name which is above every name that at the Name of Jesus every knee should bow of those in heaven, and of those on earth and those under the earth, and that every tongue should confess that Jesus Christ is Lord to the glory of God the Father."*
> [Philippians 2:9-11]

This means that a Christian has received power through the name of Jesus Christ to defeat Satan. By the divine authority given to Jesus, the battle against Satan and sin was won and won once and for all. The Name of Jesus is a victor's name. Whosoever uses the name will be delivered and have victory over all the giants of life. The name of Jesus is an assured name; and it is a blessed assurance, the name that is above every other name. [Philippians 2:9]

How to conquer your Giants

There are seven principles you can use to conquer your giants. Joseph used these seven principles to fight the giants that challenged his dream and vision of fulfilling God's plan and purpose on earth and getting to the top position God destined for him in Egypt.

1. By Godly Influence [Genesis 39:1-4]

Godly influence does not negate the opposition of the enemy. The greater it is upon your life, the more persecution and opposition you will receive from the 'giants' at all times. The opposition will come but it will not prevail over you.

2. By Fidelity [Genesis 39:5-6]

Despite Joseph's faithfulness to the work of his master, he faced the problem of false accusation and no one was on his side to support him. The order came to throw him into the prison but God used this to perfect his work of elevation and fulfilment in his life.

When God is at work in your life, He will influence the people around you to take their hands off because the situation will be divinely controlled. The help and support of human beings cannot prevent the divine assignment of God coming to pass in your life.

3. By Resisting Temptation [Genesis 39: 7-9]

Like Joseph, resisting temptation is paramount if you want to get to the next level of life. You must try your best to resist the temptation of the enemy. This will help you to achieve the divine assignment of God for your life. In the case of Joseph, though he resisted the immoral woman, she still managed to implicate him.

Whatever the strategy of the enemy might be, you will come out as a winner in the end just as Joseph did if you resist and flee from all temptations.

4. By God's Favour [Genesis 39: 20-22]

Divine favour can never be duplicated. It follows you wherever you go to complete the goodwill of God in your life. Though everyone may hate you, He will lead you to the appointed place at His appointed time.

Joseph was hated by his brothers, thrown into the pit, sold into slavery, lied against and thrown into the prison yet again; yet all the time he carried God's favour. Whatever you are passing through, if you are a child of God, you are a carrier of God's favour

5. By Divine Providence [Genesis 40:58]

He became the man in charge of Potiphar's house.

In the prison Joseph became a consultant to the other prisoners.

He was brought before Pharaoh and elevated to Prime Minister.

You should always hope for the best in any circumstance because the purpose and promise of God will happen at the right place and at the right time in your life.

6. By Honouring God [Genesis 41: 15-16]

Honouring God in your circumstances is basic if you want to achieve your God-given dreams. You must always rejoice and thank God in every situation. Joseph received wisdom from God and was always ready to glorify God and acknowledge His greatness in return for what He gave him. Once in Egypt there was no bragging or vainglory of any kind from Joseph. He considered Jehovah as the number one priority in his life.

7. By Maintaining a Relationship with God [Genesis 41: 25-36]

Joseph maintained a relationship with God in all his troubles and trials of life. He developed this from his youth as God endowed him with wisdom and revelation. Joseph was in a foreign land but did not adopt the habits and customs of the people there. He distinguished himself by his godly character. He could interact with God any time, anywhere, in any situation. Neither persecution, slavery nor imprisonment could separate Joseph from his God. No wonder he found favour with God and men. All children of God must have a solid relationship with their Father in heaven as Joseph did in order to receive the grace and favour of God in all areas of their lives.

You cannot do it on your own; your giants will defeat you anytime you tackle them in your own strength. David told Goliath:

> *"And all this assembly shall know that the Lord saves not with sword and spear; this is the Lord's battle and He will give you into our hands."*
>
> [1 Samuel 17:47]

This implies that David relied on the strength of God to defeat his giant.

You need divine help to overcome your old habits and establish new behaviours. Paul declared - *"I can do all things through Christ which strengthens me."* [Philippians 4:13] You also can confess the same to receive the support of God.

You can be freed from Giants

The type of giants individuals face are different and numerous, and can be tackled in the same way David did when he conquered the Philistine warrior.

Believing and trusting in the Lord of Hosts and His strength is paramount to winning the battle of giants.

The Bible confirmed that as Goliath moved closer to attack, David quickly ran to meet him. [1 Samuel 17:48] Similarly, do not run away; do not try to negotiate with your giant. Don't compromise nor make any excuse to back off from your giants. Force your giant out into the light and do not let him come back into your life. Establish boundaries and make yourself accountable. Stay out of the wrong company; above all, do not look at God in the light of your giant, look at your giant in the light of God who is able to do the impossible.

Whoever believes in God will be delivered and have abundant life. Your abundant life is to enjoy God-given freedom from sin and have your status changed forever to a 'winner'.

Points to note

- You can enjoy financial freedom.

- You can have marital enrichment.

- You can experience freedom from sickness.

- You can enjoy freedom to serve God as His child.

- You can use His name to receive anything your heart desires according to His will. [Mark11:24]

- Do not allow Satan to use circumstances to steal your joy. Where there is no joy, there will be no peace. Where there is no peace, a renewed mind and right thinking will become difficult.

- The circumstances that you are facing today are not peculiar to you alone, many have passed through them before. [1 Corinthians10:13]

- You should patiently and diligently run the race set before you. [Hebrews 12:1]

- God is aware of those things that happen to you which He allows in order to complete His good will for your life.

- Move away from man's traditions and allow God to grant you a new beginning.

- Assess situations with divine wisdom as they arise.

- Move away from conventional life into abundant life. Do not allow temporary events to overshadow you with clouds of doubt.

Chapter 5

The Weapons for Conquering Your Giants

The Power of the Word of God

The Word of God is an immutable source of empowerment for all children of God. Through His Word we know and identify who He is, and that His presence is with us. God can never change and His Word is inseparable from Him. If we trust in His Word, then we show that we are trusting in Him.

People may ignorantly deny the existence of God even in the face of the reality of creation. The Word declares that without a Creator, there can be no creation. [Psalm 19:1-7] Nothing was created without the spoken word of God. His Word became flesh which we saw in Jesus, who became the evidence of the Word of God.

God's Word heals the sick and makes whole everyone who believes in Him; It saves and changes lives, changes situations, revives human beings, and changes curses to blessings.

The demonstration of the power of the Word of God was seen in the earthly ministry of Jesus.

- He rebuked the wind and the wind obeyed. [Matthew 8: 26-27]

- He cursed the barren fig tree [Mark 11: 13-14] and it dried from the root.

- He destroyed every curse of life for us so that we may be blessed by the Word.

- He heals because it is part of His nature as Jehovah Rapha.

- He cast out evil spirits. [Mark 9: 21-25]

Wherever and whenever Jesus speaks, things happen to glorify the Father.

Believe and use the 'Word' of God. Let the Word work for you if you believe it is with you. We can apply the power in the Word of God the way David used it to gain confidence and faith to defeat Goliath.

The Knowledge of God

You must be sure that you are in agreement with God before using His Word. You will not enjoy the efficacy of God's Word if you are rebelling against Him by your actions.

Jesus reassures us that "... *as many as received Him, to them He gave the right to become the children of God, to those who believe in His name*" [John 1:12] so that the marvellous light of God can be revealed in them.

Jesus is the only foundation -*"For no other foundation can anyone lay than that which is laid, which is Jesus Christ."* [1 Corinthians 3:11]

Jesus said - *"I am the way, the truth and the life no one comes to the Father except through Me."* [John 14:6]

The victory is assured for you no matter how rough and tough it may be and how 'the giant' may intimidate you. It is important to cultivate an unbreakable relationship like that of David.

Points to Note

- The Scripture declares:

  "For the Word of God is quick and powerful and sharper than any two edged sword, piercing even to the dividing asunder of soul and spirit and of the joints and marrow and as a discerner of the thoughts and intents of the heart."

  [Hebrew 4:12]

- The word of God brings assurances such as the following:

  "So shall I keep Your law continually for ever and ever, and I will walk at liberty for I seek Your precepts, I will speak of Your testimonies also before kings and will not be ashamed."

  [Psalm 119:44-46]

- The Word of God brings solace, security and consolation and is a hiding place. [Psalm 91:14-16]

- *"The name of the Lord is a strong tower, the righteous run to it and are safe."* [Proverbs 18:10]

- The word of God is a seed, which when sowed will bring life. If you allow the word of God to grow and abide in your life richly, there can be no weapon formed against you that will prosper or stand. As the Bible states:

  "No weapon formed against you shall prosper, And every tongue which rises against you in judgement you shall condemn, This is the heritage of the servants of the Lord, And their righteousness is from Me, says the Lord."
  [Isaiah 54:17; Colossians 3:16]

- When you are confronted with a generation issue of life experienced by your parents or grand parents such as divorce, infertility, loneliness, poverty, anger, depression, hypertension, and addiction, face them with the word of God. Fearlessly rebuke, renounce and destroyed them once and for all.

- God has endowed you with the power of faith to use His Word to win battles.

Use the word of God systematically just

as David selected five stones to go to the battle with Goliath, the Philistine warrior. He selected his stones in good faith but only needed one.

The five stones selected may represent the following:

The Stone of Priority

David proved that there is a God in Israel, and therefore invoked His name over the situation to show His might and power over the enemy of the people of God. When David was discouraged from fighting Goliath, he made up his mind to trust God whole heartedly based on what God did in his life while he was looking after the flock of his father. [1 Samuel 17:46-47]

The Stone of Past Successes

David declared God to be his deliverer from the lion and bear and was still trusting Him for another victory over Goliath. [1 Samuel 17: 36-37] David was keeping record of God's faithfulness and His marvellous work. Indeed, so should we:

> *"Seek the Lord and His strength; seek His face evermore! Remember His marvellous works which He has done, His wonders and judgments of His mouth."*
>
> [1 Chronicles 16:11-12]

God has never failed and He will not fail you

if you trust in His unfailing power.

The Stone of Passion

You must have the passion through the Word of God to confront the enemy and win. Rehearsing your hurts won't heal the wound or solve your problems. Have strong courage and unshakable faith to defeat your enemy. Your passion in what you are doing gives you enough courage and determination to fight to win without fainting.

The Stone of Prayer

In your ongoing warfare, prayer must be very important. [Ephesians 6: 18-19] David called on God when Saul sought to kill him. Involving God in your situation gives Him plenty of opportunities to defend you for a lasting victory.

The Stone of Perseverance and Tenacity

David determined to go the distance and was fully prepared to win in the name of the Lord. It may take you longer than David, perhaps more than a month, or a year or longer to see results. But, rest assured that with God, victory is sure and all things are possible.

The Written and the Unwritten (Revealed) Word of God

The written and the revealed Word of God are God's manifestations of His love for humanity.

The written Word of God is there for you to learn, understand and obey. It is eternally settled that you can do anything the Word of God says you can do. The Word of God is there to give you help and victory in time of trouble.

The written word of God is powerful and active whenever you are ready to use it for God's righteousness purposes. This simply means that the Word of God will do whatever we want it to do as long as we are in agreement with God.

The Bible is the written Word of God and it is for all generations and needs no editing. The editor and author is God and He is all-knowing. Though we can argue that men were moved by the Holy Spirit to write, God inspired them to write what he wanted.

That is why the word of God is settled forever with Him in heaven. [Psalm 119:89] Anyone who attempts to change anything from the Bible would be doing so at his or her own peril.

Chapter 6

Equipping Yourself Against Giants

When you are born again, there is a greater power behind you. Any storm that you may be going through is taking you to your promised destiny.

> All things were made through Him; and without Him nothing was made that was made. [John 1:3]

> All authority has been given to Him in heaven and in earth. [Matthew 28:18]

> No weapon formed against you can stand or prosper. [Isaiah 54:17]

There are four principal tools which will equip you for action:

- The Name of Jesus.

- The Word of God.

- The Blood of Jesus.

- The Power of Prayer.

The Name of Jesus is an authoritative Name given by God to demolish all powers and principalities. As the Apostle Paul declared:

> "Wherefore God has highly exalted Him, and given Him a name which is above every name, that at the name of Jesus

every knee should bow, of things in heaven, and things in earth, and things under the earth and that every tongue should confess that Jesus Christ is Lord to the glory of God the Father."

[Philippians 2:9-11]

This scripture highlights a 'Name' not names, which is an indication that the name of Jesus carries promise and power. No other names can do what His name can and will do on earth and in heaven.

The name of the Lord is strong and powerful. The righteous can claim the name to be saved. The name needs to be remembered whenever there is battle lying ahead, since *"... the weapons of our warfare are not carnal but mighty in God for pulling down strongholds."* [2 Corinthians 10:4] Therefore, calling on His name silently or loudly will avail much for your benefit.

Everything that was created has a name but Jesus' name is superior to all other names. The name Of Jesus becomes efficacious and powerful in every situation. You therefore need His name to win all kinds of battles in all kinds of circumstances.

Points to note

- The name of Jesus is the only name by which humanity can be saved. The scripture confirms:

   "Neither is there salvation in any

other: for there is none other name under heaven given among men whereby we must be saved. "

[Acts 4:12 KJV]

- The name of Jesus is fire in the camp of the enemy when mentioned for deliverance. It is always good to remember to call on the name of the Lord in the days of trouble.

- Calling on the name of Jesus can change your status from a sinner to a son of God and co-heir to the promises of God.

- Calling on Jesus' name signifies that you acknowledge the pre-eminence of His name and that we as His Church have the privilege to call on Him to intervene in all areas of our lives.

- Jesus is the Son of God, and through Him you become co-heirs. [Romans 8:15-17] Life flows from God and He is the Author and Keeper of life.

The efficacy of prayer

Prayer is a means by which any Christian can walk and work with God. It is the most honourable way to communicate and receive from God.

Jesus' teachings on many occasions centred on prayer and how you can pray. The disciples wanted him to teach them how to pray and he taught them what is commonly known as The Lord's prayer. He shared a parable about an unjust judge which emphasised the importance of persevering in prayer. Jesus also said that whatever you ask for when you pray, you should believe that you have received the answer, and you will, as long as what you have asked for is consistent with His Word. [Luke 18:1; Mark 11:24-25]

All of the foregoing are indications that prayer is an integral part of the ministry that Jesus has committed to us. When you pray, God is ready to answer you through the channel of His Son. It is only through, and by the name of Jesus Christ, that the prayer of the righteous man can be answered.

In the past, people did pray and their prayers were answered. Since God is same yesterday, today, and tomorrow, if we persist in prayer, He will also answer us today.

Remember to pray by the authority of God's Word and follow its precepts.

Jesus in His Word

Prayer is the power source behind the growth of the early Church. They prayed constantly, including before the day of Pentecost and afterwards with startling results. The Scripture confirmed:

"With great power, the apostles were

*testifying to the resurrection of the Lord
Jesus Christ, and much grace was upon
them all. "*

[Acts 4:33]

And more and more men and women
came to believe in the Lord Jesus Christ
and were added to them. [Acts 5:14] There
is a strong relationship between prayer,
the Word of God and the righteousness
and growth of the Church.

We read in Acts that *"Peter was kept in
prison, but the Church was earnestly
praying to God for him. "* [Acts 12:5] Prayer
is the only power which the powerless
possess. You can fight against the enemy
with the Sword of the Spirit [Ephesians 6:17]
and with determination and intensity in
prayer.

They prayed before selecting and
appointing leaders, during times of
persecution and also for the progress of
the gospel. [Acts 6:1-7]

Prayer demonstrates your dependence
on God. You cannot build the Church in
your own strength. [Psalm 127:1] Human
beings can build organisations and clubs
and institutions with their knowledge
and intelligence; but only God can build
the Church. Jesus promised to build his
Church against which the gates of hell will
not prevail. [Matthew 16:18]

Prayer is the power source behind all

Church health and growth, and must not be neglected.

You should not rely on your ability to do things but rely on God through the teaching of His Word, sermons and various ways of praying encouraged in all facets of the Church's activities.

The Church should model dynamic praying, starting from the pastor and extending to all other leaders and church workers. Large segments of time should be devoted to praying despite their busy schedules.

Pastors and preachers should spend more time praying about their sermons than preparing them. Talking to God about the impact of His Word in the lives of the hearers is a major part of preparation. They must engender accountability for the prayer life of the Church.

We must make prayer an indispensable tool in understanding the vision of God for the Churches. Not only must we look beyond the world's ideas of what the vision should be, we must also look beyond the vision of other Churches, since the vision God gives to one Church is not the same as to another. May God miraculously open our eyes to His plans and purposes for our churches.

The prayers of the early leaders unleashed the power of God to add thousands of souls to the Church. For example, it was said of the Apostles John and Peter that:

"... when they had prayed, the place where they were assembled together was shaken; and they were filled with Holy Spirit, and they spoke the Word of God with boldness."

[Acts 4:31]

It can surely happen in our Churches today.

We must pray for spiritual and numerical growth because it is God's will for the Church to be healthy and prosper. A healthy Church will attract people of all races and ages.

Church leaders ought to set the pace

When prayer is at the heart of Church leaders at all levels, this will be seen in their lives and their personal contributions and eventually transform the church at large. We must encourage significant periods of prayer at the meetings of workers, and at the various team conferences and committees of all groups in the life of the Church.

Prayer must characterise all aspects of the Church's ministry for effective demolition of giants in the Church of God. The ministers of God must inspire the Church to believe in God and depend on Him for success in all areas of their lives.

David decimated the giant Goliath by trusting in the God of Israel to fight and assist him to conquer this boastful enemy of Israel.

The power praise

Be sure that you give Him praise in return for responding to and His answers to your prayers. God deserves to have your praise and worship. He is God and there is no other way you can demonstrate your gratitude for His greatness other than through praise and worship.

You worship God to remind yourself that He is the great God and the only person in your life who deserves you total surrender. You also show through your praise and worship that all things come from Him.

The people did not know how powerful their praise and worship was until they saw the wall of Jericho, which they thought would be a barrier on their way, come down.

Do not look at the mountain or giant before you but rather check the staff in your hand. What you have and the Word in your mouth is enough for you to defeat your giants and receive your victory.

Being steadfast in Christ Jesus

You will not achieve your destiny without facing troubles. Never be inwardly troubled when trouble is troubling you. [2 Corinthians 4:8-9]

God assured Joshua - *"No man shall stand before you in every place the sole of your foot shall tread."* [Joshua 1:1-5] This was an unconditional promise for Joshua who had surrendered to Jehovah as His servants.

Joseph's brothers plotted against him in so many ways yet Joseph didn't praying against them who were against him. He even forgave them when they came to him for help. [Genesis 50:20-21]

Born-again, Spirit-filled believers are seated with Christ in the heavenly places above power and principality. [Ephesians 1:3-11] They function from a position of victory in Christ with the will of God in their hearts.

The battle of your life belongs to the Lord. The Word of God says we walk under the authority of the Lord - it is not a physical fight; therefore stand firm in the Lord against your giant. Learn how to stand while you are doing the will of God. Apostle Paul encouraged us:

"Therefore take up the whole armour of God, that you may be able to withstand in the evil day, and having done all, to stand ... above all taking the shield of faith with which you will be able to quench all the fiery darts of the wicked

one."

[Ephesians 6:13-16 selected]

You only need to fight in faith. In spiritual warfare, you need to maintain your faith in God through His word. There is a wrestle in life that operates through the flesh and blood but extends into spiritual powers and realities. You should not do anything less or more, or teach anything less or more than what the Bible teaches in order to put on the armour of God, then resist the devil by being steadfast in faith.

The idea of fighting the devil is popular today in some Christian gatherings by reference to physical and animistic practices [based on the belief that animals and plants may possess a demonic spirit]. Many Christians believe that we should glean knowledge and tactics from pagan tradition or beliefs to fight the devil, and we need pagan based spiritual weapons to defeat him. However God's Word has the power to withstand every erroneous belief.

Resist the Devil

"Submit yourselves therefore to God. Resist the devil, and he will flee from you."

[James 4:7]

To resist the devil means to say 'no' to all his advances, deceptions and ways. In other words, it means to disagree with the devil and his agents in all areas of your life.

When the enemy tries to lie to you in various ways, you resist the enemy by being steadfast in the word of God and in your faith. It must be 'God says' and not what man thinks and says. The Word of God must richly dwell in you, strengthening your inner man to withstand all the evils of this age. [Colossians 3:16]

Only thinking in line with what the Bible says, is what will make you a winner. Do not be a negative thinker but rather be positive in your thinking according to the Word of God. *"For as he thinks in his heart, so is he…"* [Proverbs 23:7] To be a winner in spiritual warfare, you must be ready to think scripturally and walk spiritually in line with Christ.

Do not let your mind fall into superstitions that are handed down from generation to generation and which are not in agreement with the Word of God.

Be focused and fight the fight of faith

"Fight the good fight of faith, lay hold on eternal life, where unto thou art also called, and have professed a good profession before many witnesses."
[1 Timothy 6:12; 2 Timothy 4:7 KJV]

You can fight the good fight of faith by:

- Keeping God's ordinances or His commandments.

- Not faltering or drawing back due to temptations, persecutions or diversions.

- Holding fast to the faith and the Word of God.

- Putting on the full armour of God.

- Pressing forward each day doing the will of God.

There will be opposition to those who truly believe in God, [2 Timothy 3:12] but you must press forward towards the mark of the high calling of God in Christ Jesus. [Philippians 3:14] You must live in dependence on God and His provisions. Though the Bible says *"Ye are gods"* [Psalm 82:6; John 10:34 KJV], you cannot create things or try to create things after your own will or lusts. This simply means we are representatives of God in whatever He directs us to do.

You are an ambassador of Christ, who delivers the Word of God which God then confirms with signs. You can only benefit from God's instruction by following and trusting His Word. [2 Corinthians 5:20]

Be obedient to God and His Word

You should always remember that the fight and battle is not yours, it belongs to the Lord. The Lord is backing you; therefore, you can move forward in confidence with praises in your mouth to win your battles. [2 Chronicles 20:15]

The Lord gives instructions and it must be followed to gain victory. His ways are not your ways and your thoughts are not His. The foolishness of God is wiser than the wisdom of men; and His weakness is stronger than the strength of men in all their ways. [Isaiah 55:8, 1 Corinthians 1:25]

The route God has chosen for you is purposeful and unique for you to secure victory. *"God has chosen the foolish things of the world to put to shame the wise, and God has chosen the weak things of the world to put to shame the things which are mighty."* [1 Corinthians 1:27] This is evident in the case of the Israelites demolishing the wall of Jericho in the simplest of ways imaginable.

If you are going to receive all you ask from God, you must be ready to trust and obey His simple instructions. When God speaks, He means what He says and He says, what He means, for your benefit. Therefore the words of God are infallible.

It takes a great deal of humility to listen to, to trust in and to obey the God you cannot see. Jesus revealed God to us and the Holy Spirit interprets the nature of God to those who are ready to submit to His will.

You should never be proud of anything other than what God has accomplished in Christ Jesus. He is the only true way of achieving the objectives for your life. Therefore, humbly accept what Apostle John says - *"A man can receive nothing unless it has been given to him from heaven."* [John 3:27]

Chapter 7

Destroying Your Personal Giants

The destruction of giants must start with you before you can help others to do the same. Jesus said:

> "Why behold thou the mote that is in thy brother's eye, but consider not the beam that is in thine own eye?"
>
> [Matthew 7:3 KJV]

The truth is that many call themselves 'deliverance ministers' while they are yet to be delivered from the works of the devil; they are messengers of the devil and angels of darkness.

Jesus came to give light, because He is the Light and insight for you to see and know which way to go. He is *"the way and the truth and the life."* When you choose to follow him, you cannot walk in darkness.
[John 1:5; 14:6]

When you follow Jesus and live daily according to His truth, you walk in the light; those who walk in the light through Jesus who is the 'Light of the world', can easily show others how to live in the light. You are to be salt and light in this world and this means that you can instruct the world especially those who are yet to come to the knowledge of God through Christ Jesus.

[Matthew 5:13-14]

To destroy your personal giants, you need to take the following four steps:

1. Forget Your Past Sin

Sin is a burden in life which has been cleansed by the blood of Jesus Christ. The framework by which it has to be cleansed was laid down by Jesus Christ himself through His death and resurrection. Whenever you accept Christ Jesus as your Lord and Saviour through the confession of your sins and the acceptance of Jesus' death on the cross for the atonement of your sins, Jesus' redeeming blood automatically does the rest which you cannot do. Your sins are forgiven and you are free indeed. Don't try to remember those sins that the blood of Jesus has cleansed from your life.

The promises of Jehovah God are instant and solid. God said *"I, even I, am He that blot out thy transgressions for My own sake; And I will not remember your sins."* [Isaiah 43:25 KJV] You may change your words often because of circumstances that are beyond your control. In the case of God, He is never controlled by any circumstance but He is in control of all storms of life. He determines the end of any matter before it even occurs. [Isaiah 46:10]

What you need to do is to see the

superiority of God in all your situations; He says what He does and He does what He says He will do. You can never forgive and cleanse your own sin. Jesus atoned for your sins by the cleansing power of His blood.

The blood of Jesus Christ has been shed for the atonement of your sins and that is the end of the matter. God has forgiven you and you should therefore forget your past sins that have been forgotten by God; only He can lay a charge against you in the first place for your sins.

Therefore, if the Lord is for you, nothing can any longer against you. [Romans 8:31] Stop dwelling on your past mistakes. God loves mankind and revealed this in His Son:

> *"He who did not spare His Son, but delivered Him up for us all, how not with Him also freely give us all things?"*
> [Romans 8:31-32]

2. Forget Your Past and Present Positions

You should use your present position to glorify God for what He has in store for you. The simple reason that you are alive is an indication that God is preparing a better tomorrow for you to reshape things to the glory of God.

No one can change the past except God who existed before time began and shall continue to exist forever. You cannot change your past. Therefore, you should not let any experience, either past or present, influence your thinking about what has already happened.

"There is a time for every purpose under the sun." [Ecclesiastes 3:1] There is a time of turbulence and trouble that will eventually lead to triumph. Keep looking unto your Creator who is the Author of all good things in your life.

Live your life by the grace of the Son of God. The Apostle Paul said:

"I have been crucified with Christ and I no longer live, but Christ lives in me. The life I live in the body, I live by faith in the Son of God, who loved me and gave himself for me."

[Galatians 2:20]

Always see your life as a testimonial of the wonderful work of God and stop dwelling on your past glories or miseries. Your tomorrow is better than what you wrongly thought of yourself in the past.

Jehovah God has better plans for you:

"... thoughts of peace, and not of evil, to give you a future and a hope."

[Jeremiah 29:11]

Be more inspired by your tomorrow than your past. Therefore never look at your circumstances to the detriment of what God has prepared to release into your life. God wants you to be a source of blessing to others, and hence He allows you to pass through trials of life that seem unpleasant in order to bring you to a better future.

3. Stop Worrying About Your life

Jesus said:

"... do not worry about your life, what you will eat or what you will drink; nor about your body, what you will put on. Is not life more than food and the body more than clothing?"

[Matthew 6:25]

Worries can do more damage than good in your life. Because of worry, many people end up with compounded problems. The object of their worry consumes their thoughts thereby obstructing any productive insight. Your worries can have a negative effect on the way you treat others and lead to jealousy and envy.

Your worries can drastically reduce your ability to trust in God and disrupt your progress in life:

"Be anxious for nothing; but in everything by prayer and supplication with thanksgiving let your requests be made known to God."

[Philippians 4:6]

In conclusion, believe in God and His Word, and continue praying by faith, always believing that you will receive His answers to your prayers.

4. Press On To Maturity

Christian maturity leads you to attain the heights of your life which God wants you to achieve.

Your maturity enables you to apply the principles of Christianity and live out those principles in practice. You should effectively live your daily life for Christ and depend on Him.

Do not live your life in the past; Jesus came to rectify your past that you might have peace with God and look forward for a better tomorrow. If you have anything on your mind that is causing you to doubt your relationship with God, seek the reassurance of His promise.

If you forget the past and press forward to the attainment of a better future in the Lord, then this goal should absorb all your energy and keep you from becoming distracted.

Therefore, follow Christ with single-mindedness and lay aside every harmful weight and forsake anything that may distract you from being an effective Christian. Your hope should be in Christ and you should let go of the past guilt and look forward to what God will help you to become in the future.

Do not dwell on your past. Instead, grow in the knowledge of God and concentrate on your relationship with Jesus who will perfect all things concerning you. Realise that you have been forgiven and move on to a life of faith and obedience to God. Press on and look forward to a fuller, more meaningful and productive life with your hope resting on Jesus Christ and his love for you.

Chapter 8

Fighting and Overcoming the Giants of Your Mind

As we are approach the conclusion of this book, the significance of fighting and winning the battles of life especially the battles of the mind, should be getting clearer.

Your mind or your soul is the workshop which your brain, the conductor of the activities of your life, relies on to send messages to other parts of your body. This enables you to operate in a functional state of mind in your environment. Therefore, if your soul prospers and is in good health, you can also be prosperous in rational thinking.

The day you start thinking positively and rightly about your life, it will bring you to the verge of your breakthrough in life. The activities and achievements in your life are based on the power of your perception. This means that you can clearly visualise, will eventually lead to the actualisation of your life's dreams; in other words, your perception plus your rational thinking can lead to positive action.

You should be careful not to let your perception of things destroy God's promises for your life. What you see, what you think, how you feel about things around you and what people say, should not be allowed to contradict the promise of God for your life. The promises of God are always intact and will surely come to pass despite any uncomfortable incidents that may arise.

Christianity is not a trouble-free venture

Christianity is not an easy way of life but will often bring trouble to your doorstep. The Bible warns us that:

> *"Those who want to live a godly life in Christ will suffer persecution."*
>
> *[2 Timothy 3:12]*

God will take you through the ordeal and eventually deliver you. He will not forsake you or leave you defeated. He is always by your side as promised, both in the waters and fires of life. [Isaiah 43:1-2]

Trouble is not limited to any particular gender, race, religion or home. For *"everyone born of a woman is of few days and full of troubles."* [Job 14:1-2]

Job went from the fullness of God's blessings to the position of suffering hardship, then back to enjoying the fullness of God's blessings. God will surely release you from all your captivities if you trust in Him.

Paul was changed from Saul to Paul, and from being puffed up with knowledge and arrogance to a humble apostle who had to endure great troubles and trials but nevertheless with the assurance of a crown of life.

Troubles will come your way but you must have the courage, knowledge, tenacity and principles for conquering and destroying the root of troubles and strongholds in your life.

The pillar upon which your troubles and winning ways rest is the death and resurrection of our Lord Jesus Christ. He went through much greater troubles than what you are going through in life; He prayed and spoke the Word and stood on the Word of God and that was how He conquered.

Seven Ways of Winning Against these Giants

1. Trouble will Lead to Triumph and Testimony

Do not be intimidated by trouble. Remember the ten spies among the twelve who went to survey the Promised Land - they foolishly lost out on what could, with God's help, have been an easy possession. [Numbers13:26-33]

Without trouble, there will be no testimonial and you can never get to your promised destination. There is no destiny achieved without trouble encountered - Jesus being a prime example. He was betrayed and was denied but He triumphed beyond any man who ever lived.

2. When Trouble Troubles You, Don't be

Troubled

Never be troubled when trouble troubles you but remember that *"many are the afflictions of the righteous but the Lord delivers him from them all."* [Psalm 34:19] God is interested in your troubles. *"He is your refuge and strength, and He is a very present help in trouble."* [Psalm 46:1]

3. Remember to Use Your Weapons

Do not throw away your weapons when you are hurt by troubles. Refrain from shifting blame and passing the buck. Jesus was tempted yet without sin. He will give you victory because He has gone through it before and did not fail. [Hebrew 2:18; 4:15]

4. Remember to Pray and Cry to the Lord for Help

What you say in the midst of trouble matters so much. [Psalm 107:19-20] Speak the Word in faith with courage and strength. [Joshua 1:6-7] Speak to the stronghold or mountain the Word of God and rely on His promises with a positive attitude of expectation.

5. Cast Down Evil Imaginations [2 Corinthians 10:5]

Stop being negative about your life and be a positive thinker and speaker. Do not allow evil thoughts that are never in line with the Word of God to overshadow the purpose of God in your life. You should remember that Jehovah has good thoughts about you. Therefore, the trouble you are facing will not stop the promise, purpose and plan of God for your life. [Jeremiah 29:11]

Pray for all aspects of your life - spouse, children, business, education, career, church, and yourself. Cast down evil imaginations in prayers with the Word of God. Learn how to accept forgiveness for yourself which you have received through the blood of Jesus, and forgive others in order to receive the best and perfect gift from God, for there is no forgiveness without forgiving. [Matthew 6:15]

Those who cannot forgive those who have wronged them of their wrongs and will not let go of the past wrong done to them, are inviting Satan back into their lives. Paul wrote:

" ...that I might put you to the test, whether you are obedient in all things. Now whom you forgive anything I also forgive, for if indeed I have forgiven anything, I have forgiven that one for your sakes in the presence of Christ, lest Satan should take advantage of us; for we are not ignorant of his devices."
[2 Corinthians 2:9-11]

6. Be Spirit-Filled

Ask for the Holy Spirit and to be filled with Him and nothing else. He will guide you to the perfect plan and purpose of God for your life. Jesus wants you to ask for the Holy Spirit so that you can receive Him. [Luke 11:13]

7. Be Humble and Obedient [Ecclesiastes 12:13]

Obedience is simply doing and surrendering to the commandment of God no matter what the result may bring even when you are tempted to do to the contrary.

Do not try to change or twist the Word of God to favour your wilful inclinations. Therefore do as the Word of God says. We can never know better than God His decisions always bring great results.

Obedience is the greatest weapon to fight and conquer the giants of the mind. Whatever you imagine in your mind comes to action in your life, but if you believe in the Word of God that you confess, you will surely win. You must give Jesus complete obedience to be a winner.

Let the fighting and overcoming of the giants of your mind start from your thinking; see the wall of Jericho that is before you as a fallen wall by faith; think positively, act positively and overcoming your giants will be certain.

You should always remember that you are fighting against a defeated enemy; therefore, you must have confidence in God's words. Your enemy has been defeated by Jesus Christ. Therefore, do not create another artificial giant for yourself. [Romans 8:37-38, Hebrew 2:14, 1 John 3:8]

Although you fight spiritual battles everyday and sin runs rampant in the world, you must have the assurance that the battle has already been won. You do not have to be paralysed by the craftiness of a defeated giant by allowing him to control your thinking and mindset. You are more than a conqueror through the power of Christ Jesus. [Romans 8:37]

Conclusion

To defeat your giants, you must accept Jesus Christ as your Lord and Saviour. He is the Creator, the life-giver and the law-giver, who intervenes in the course of your life whenever you call on Him in times of trouble. God still answers the prayers of His people. Although God is loving and merciful, He has clearly outlined in His Word two contrasting ways of dealing with humanity. He is the God of justice and judgement who rewards us according to our works. He gives us the opportunity to make choices and allows us to reap whatever we sow.

This book has hopefully helped you to understand what life is all about, and learn to make the right choices that will bring the lasting reward of defeating the giants in your life.

God alone is the One who gives victory over giants. In the case of David and Goliath, David defeated the arrogant and pompous Philistine through his faith in what God would do. God will be pleased to see the changes in your life after the defeat of your giants.

Remember what the Bible says:

"The weapons of our warfare are not carnal, but mighty through God to the pulling down of strongholds casting down imagination and every high thing

that exalt itself against the knowledge of God, and bringing into captivity every thoughts to the obedience of Christ."

[2 Corinthians 10:4]

God's mighty weapons are available to you as you fight against Satan's strongholds. As a Christian, you must choose between God's methods and the World's methods. Never forget that the world's methods will fail you. David rejected the worldly weapons and armour of Saul but relied on Jehovah God of Israel for victory.

You are assured in the Bible that God's mighty weapons - prayer, faith, hope, love, God's word, and the Holy Spirit - are powerful and effective weapons to defeat all the giants you will face in life. [Ephesians 6:13-18]

The life of king David is a testament to how God's children can conquer their giants with His help. Trust God like David and Abraham and you too will have victory and 'Defeat Your Giants'.

www.ingramcontent.com/pod-product-compliance
Lightning Source LLC
Chambersburg PA
CBHW070107070426
42448CB00038B/1840